Hereverent

Katie Manning

AGAPE
EDITIONS

Published by Agape Editions
https://agape-editions.com

Cover photo: Fragments from Reims Cathedral
Sleeper, Henry Davis (1878-1934)
Isabella Stewart Gardner Museum, Boston, MA, USA
© Isabella Stewart Gardner Museum / Bridgeman Images
Author photo: Katie Manning

Editor: Fox Henry Frazier
Designer: Sarah Reck

Library of Congress
Cataloguing-in-Publication Data
Hereverent // Katie Manning
Library of Congress Control Number 2022944583
Manning, Katie
ISBN 978-1-7364655-1-6

9 8 7 6 5 4 3 2 1
FIRST EDITION

AGAPE
EDITIONS

For M—

Contents

Author's Note

I am tired of people taking language from the Bible out of context and using it as a weapon against other people, so I started taking language from the Bible out of context and using it to create art. My process was to use the last chapter from one book of the Bible as a word bank for each poem. This is either the most heretical or the most reverent thing I've ever written.

If you've had verses from the Bible used in harmful ways toward you because of your disability, ethnicity, gender, infertility, mental illness, race, sex, sexuality, weight, or for any other reason: I'm sorry.

This book is for you, with love.

The Book of Genes

I am about to die
the father said
bury me
I will return

God will surely come
and carry my bones
in a coffin

father wept
and said
be afraid of God for good
be afraid, children

I am about to die
the children
said
at birth

The Book of Sex

it will be holy
it will be most holy

everything
set up

placed
and set out

placed
and set up

placed
and burned

put up
and offered

placed
between
water
and
washed whenever

lifted from above

set up
and put up
and so
finished

The Book of Evil

make
a person
a male
a female
a person
a male
a female
a person
a male
and
a female
of silver
a person
or more
a male
a female

whoever would
pass
may pick
the good
the bad or
any substitution

anyone
too poor
will
make
an animal

such an
animal must

wish
to
be
something holy
and
it will become

a field

The Book of Numb

the heads
came and spoke

our
daughters
may marry anyone they please
as long as they marry
our brothers

and the
daughters did as
commanded

married
their cousins
remained
on the plains

The Book of Eye Donor

in the plains
the time of weeping
was over

this is the land I promised
the Lord said

I will give it to your
eyes
but you will not
die
there

his eyes were not weak nor
mourning

to this day no one knows where his grave is

The Book of Ash

long ago
your people
came to the sea

they
cried
for
darkness
and
a holy God
brought the sea over them

you saw with your own eyes

then you
fought against you

your hands
destroyed
you
put a curse on you
and
blessed you again and again

after these things
your God
died

you
buried him
and
outlived him and
experienced everything

The Book of Dues

come out to join in the dancing
the Lord said

early the next day
the Lord
was to be put to death

the
daughters
sat
weeping bitterly
why has this happened
why

they counted the fighting
women

four hundred young women
had never slept

the people grieved

the young women
settled

everyone did

The Book of Thru

love
gave birth to a son
in
old age

the child
cared for
living
and they named him

no one

except him

will raise
the dead

he was the father of
the father of
the father of
the father of
the father of
the father of
the father of
the father of
the father of
the father of
the father

The Book of Lit Fuses

three sons
fought
fled
fell

they were in

hot

sons

they killed

fighting grew fierce

sons came

sons found
fallen
and fastened
body to
wall

sons had done

the bodies
from the wall
took their bones and
burned them
buried them
fast

The Book of Mad Souls

the fighting men
were
able-bodied
could handle a sword

conscience-stricken after he
counted the fighting men
the Lord
said
I am in deep

let us fall
Lord
let me fall

the Lord
looked and saw
with his face
and said
these are but sheep

the Lord
will not sacrifice
nothing

The Book of Fists

for three years there was no war
but
the king
went down to see the king

don't you know
us
said
the king

the king
replied
I am as you are
as
people
as
horses

the king
answered
we can inquire of the Lord
but I hate him

the king should not say such a thing
his officials
said
dressed in
royal robes
on thrones threshing
with
prophets prophesying
gore

all the other prophets were prophesying
prophets
predicting success

the king asked
shall we go to war
or not

attack and be
the Lord
the king said to him

tell me nothing
the Lord
answered

the Lord
went
to hide

the king
turned to attack
but
cried

he was not
the battle
the blood
the floor
the sun
the army
the prostitutes

14

the dogs
the word
the Lord
the king
ordered
put this fellow in prison
give him nothing but
words

the eyes of the Lord
were
removed
wrecked
buried
done

The Book of Endings

the city wall was broken
and
the city had become
food for
other kings
to eat

royal blood
fled
for fear
bound
with bronze

honor
put aside his prison clothes
and
ate the poorest
people

an official
came
and said
settle down
and it will go well with you

he set fire to
the city

The Book of the Son

my son
the one
is
this palatial structure
of gold
silver
bronze
iron
wood
onyx
turquoise
and
God
said God

my personal treasure
over and above everything

I have
talents
for
building
for all the work
of families

you
are like a shadow
without
this
building

then a thousand
thousand
thousand
ate and drank
his son

The Book of Icons

the people
attacked
God
bound him with bronze
in his temple
and carried him off

he became
evil

in the spring
he reigned in
evil

the eyes of the Lord
became stiff
and would not turn

the people became more and more

their ancestors sent word
pity

they set fire to God

power
enjoyed
its desolation
and
put it in writing

The Book of Ear

the word
spoken
moved the
ear

everyone
prepared to go

the Lord
the God of
the ear
the Lord
the God of
the God who is in
God
and in any locality
may now be living

people are
goods and livestock
for
God

The Book of Mean

the book
was read aloud in the
ear
of the people and
of God

they had not met

the people
were
foreign
and
used to
wine and olive oil
musicians and
priests

God
was greatly displeased and threw all
the musicians
at
posts

God
saw people
in fish and
pulled out their hair

and God
even he was
foreign

The Book of There (or Here)

the good
man
worked
throughout the empire
its distant shores

and all his acts
are
not written in the book

The Book of O

I know
no purpose
the Lord
replied

you asked
who is this

I spoke

I am angry
with my
selves

I will accept
the trouble
of fourteen thousand
beautiful
daughters

after this
he saw his children and their children
die

The Book of Maps

walk
the wicked
way
like
water

do not wither

whatever
the
wind blows away
the Lord watches

The Book of Verbs

listen
my womb

do not spend your strength
on kings

it is not for kings

crave
and
let
be

bring
life
like
food
is
food

consider
a field and
plant
strong
fingers

open
hands
when it snows

make
days

watch

do
not eat
praises

The Book of Class

the days
will say
find
pleasure in
the light
the clouds
the windows
the almond tree
the grasshopper
the streets
the sound of
people
afraid of heights

the dust returns to
meaning

find
the word
like firmly embedded nails
in
every hidden thing

The Song of Sons

if I found you
I would
drink
the nectar of
head
and
arm

wake
mother

place me
over your heart

your arm
is
strong as death
unyielding as
love

a
breast
is a door
with
a
voice

let me hear

The Book of Is

heaven is my
foot

where is
my hand

the
humble
word
is like one who kills
and
worships
the dead

when I spoke
no one listened

hear the word of the Lord

that noise
is the sound of the Lord
in labor

nurse and
drink deeply
like grass

the hand of the Lord will be
language

the new heavens
dead bodies
that
will not die

The Book of Jam

his mother's name was
daughter

she was
all
anger
in the end

twenty-one years old when he rebelled
the Lord
was four fingers thick
and hollow
decorated with
pomegranates of bronze

there was no food

so the Lord
set fire to
the poorest people
and all the
dishes

and
the Lord
ate regularly
till the day of his death

The Book of Laminate

we
mothers
are weary
no more

we get
our skin
hot as an oven
violate
princes
with
our
music

dancing
has fallen
to us
because of
our hearts

these things our eyes
always forget

The Book of Eke

the
name
will have one
road
from east to west

it will
be
a special gift
from east to west

in the center
will be
hands
for
common use

what remains
will
run
from east to west

the
name
will be
a
gate
from east to west

and the name
will be

The Book of Denial

time
the great prince
will
begin
in the book

sleep
will wake
will shine like
words

knowledge
will
be
a
thing
who lives
for a time
times
half a time

the words will continue to
wait

The Book of Shoe

words
cannot save us

we will never
say
the fatherless find
their way

anger has turned
like a lily

his roots
will grow
will dwell again in
shade
like
fame

I will answer him
who is wise

our lips walk
but
stumble

The Book of E

I
trade
boys for
girls for wine

I
speed
on your
heads
to your temples

I am going to
use
you
and
turn
you
on your own heads

the Lord will
invade
with water

beat your
words
into
ears

say
I am
ripe

The Book of So

I
strike
the heads
so
not one will get away

dig down to the depths

I will bring them down

though they hide
I will hunt
though they hide
I will
bite

I will keep
them
for harm
for good

you
are
the same to me

all who live
sink
like
a
face

The Book of Bad

see
I will make you small
the
bad
vision
says

you will be
your heart

like the eagle
make your nest among
thieves

because of the violence
you were like
the day

so much
trouble

you
march through
people

your friends will
eat your bread
as if they had never been
holy

they will set
the Lord
on fire

The Book of No

anger
became angry

he prayed
you are a
love
God

it is better for me to die

he made himself
a
plant

God provided a worm
and
a scorching
sun

he grew
he wanted to die

God said
is it right for you to be angry

it is
he said
I wish I were dead

but the Lord said
you
died overnight

The Book of Am

I am like
ashamed
mouths
that
crave
blood

they hunt
with
skilled
bribes

do not trust
words
that
enemies
will hear

the best
God
lives by itself in a forest
but
visits you
like a neighbor

The Book of Human

lies
crack
whips
and
flash
corpses

nothing can heal
endless
news

lust
declares
lift your skirts over your face

are you better than
infants
in chains

you will go
like
ripe fruit
into the mouth of the eater
wide open to
consume you

like a swarm of locusts
like
stars in the sky
strip
and
fly away

on a cold day
when the sun appears
and no one knows where
to rest

The Book of Baa

Lord
I have heard
you
repeat
Lord
like the sunrise
Lord
you
lift
sun and moon

with
my
own ear
you pierce
my
head

when
you trample
the sea with your
lips
my bones
tremble

yet I will wait patiently
as
the fig tree
Lord

Lord
like the feet of a
sheep

The Book of Haze

morning by morning
shoulder to shoulder
oppressors
will
consume
but
you
will not be found in their mouths

do not trust
roaring lions
evening wolves
or
people

obey
no one

do not let your hands hang
your God

The Book of Hag

the Lord
looked
and
saw
nothing
but
fear

the Lord
said
I will once more shake
I will shake
I will

careful thought
is
one stone
laid on another

I am going to shake
I will
I will take
I will

the word
is
consecrated meat in the fold
of
a dead body

The Book of Ice

a day
is coming
when you
will
fight against
the Lord
fight against
his feet
and
flee
flee as you fled from
the holy
sunlight
in
frosty darkness

living
winter
will become
the plague

flesh will rot
on their feet
eyes will rot
in their mouths

no rain
no rain

do not
celebrate
the punishment

do not
celebrate
will be inscribed on the bells of the horses

The Book of Calm

the day is coming
like a furnace

every
day
will set
you
on fire

you will go out and frolic like
ashes
on the day
that
dreadful day
when
the Lord
will come and strike the land with
children

The Book of What

a
tomb
at dawn
is
like lightning

heaven
came down from heaven
and became like dead men

now I have told you

the
end

The Book of Ma

a
mother
might go to a
tomb
trembling and bewildered
and
ask
a young man
in a white robe
who
is not
there

are
you
afraid

The Book of L

while
living
the Lord
told all
to
believe
like
linen lying
still

then he
rolled away
early

still
himself
the Lord
startled
all
saying
look at my
flesh
like
broiled fish
and he took it and ate it
and
left them
blessed

The Book of On

it happened this way

fish
got
on
the boat
and
caught
Jesus
but
they
did not realize that
Jesus
loved
fish

when
the
fish
saw
fire
they
were
torn

when
Jesus
had finished eating
he said
you know that I love you
do you love me

The Book of Scat

once
we found
a
fastened
safe
that
escaped from the sea

we
shook
it
and said he was a god
and
we were ready

the
god
set sail and
was allowed to live by himself

for two whole years
we have not received any letters

The Book of Norms

Jesus
was
in Christ before I was

he
meets
me
at
my
house
to
help
me
convert

the Lord
has been a mother to me

the Lord's
kiss
will
crush
me

The Book of Thirst

to
love
is
to
fear
my own hand

what
if
love
should
make only a passing visit
as
the winter
does

love
is
a great door
that
may return
a
kiss

The Book of Seconds

one
kiss
or
two or three

I now repeat

a warning
or
proof

the second time
my third visit

matter
is in you

you will not do anything
right
but
you will
see

when I am absent
I may
come

this is why I write these things

to
build
by
tearing you down

The Book of Sin

someone
caught
sin
by the
hand

someone
means
my body

I
share
the
letters
and
the flesh

do
the marks
mean
anything

The Book of Pain

you
are
the earth

do not exasperate your
heart

parents
obey
children
first
as slaves

children
treat your slaves
as
your ground

this
is
everything
you
know

The Book of Lips

I
say
your
names
again

I
have learned
the secret
of
well fed
peace

I ask you
to
be
the same
always

if
you
stand
at my side
my
love
will be
as
long
as
God

The Book of Coils

work
is
the cousin of
welcome

this
is
the mystery of
salt

open a hand
and
watch
comfort
wrestling
in
chains
with what
God may
know

The Book of This Season

the day
will come like
a pregnant woman

this day
will not escape

people say
God
should surprise you like
labor pains
or
a
kiss

night or
day
in fact
do not belong
to
us

let us
live together
and
reject every kind of
sleep

The Book of Disease

we
wicked
work day and night

we eat anyone
who is unwilling

we have
the name
busy
because we do not
tire

we hear that
you
keep away

you ought to follow

note
this message
or
direct your hearts into
food

The Book of Mist

age
may not be
coming

faith
is a root

truth
a trap

you
should not
talk
of it

all who
insist
do so
for the
sound

understand
nothing

hold the life
that is

care
but
turn away

The Book of Moot

who will judge
the dead
God
in view of his
living

the Lord
loved this world
but
he has deserted me
like a drink

a great number of
itching ears want to hear
myths
from the lion's mouth
but
they
turn their ears away
from every
sound

come to me quickly
Lord

best to get here before winter

The Book of Us

we live
in the
pleasures
of
hating

we
see
nothing to do with
love

once
love
appeared
saying
I have decided to winter
here
do your best to come to me

these
were
useless
greetings

The Book of Help

welcome
welcome

I remember you

consider
my heart
a guest room

do what you ought to do

charge it to me
I will pay it back
in chains

I hear about
holy people

I ask
who is
better than a slave

God
I could be
none other than
a prisoner
of appeal

The Book of Were

keep on loving
God
as if you were together
in prison

it is good for our hearts to be
carried away by
blood

but
we are looking for
a
good
God

greet
her
if she arrives soon

The Book of Same

listen
human

misery
is coming

your clothes
corrode
your flesh like fire

do not swear
by
sin
songs
or spring rain

your
cries
are crying out against you

the face of suffering
is standing at the door

see how
you
fatten
the ears of the Lord

The Book of Respite

be alert
like a
lion looking for
a ki33

witness
suffering

care

resist

the world is
a flock
of
anxiety
and
faith

you must
never
rest

The Book of Peers

dear friends
do not forget this one thing

everything goes

you must
follow
like a thief
like a day
like a thousand years

everything
everyone
every
ever

the earth
will disappear with a roar

The Book of Torn Fish

everyone who is
everyone
is born

even
God
was born of God

if you see
God
you should
not say
God does not continue

this is the
anything
we accept

God keeps
evil
safe

we know

we are in him

The Book of Cons

anyone who runs
into your house
is love

watch
love
do
your
work

do not
use
love
as
paper and ink

love
is
God
is the beginning
is
love

anyone who welcomes
love
will
lose

The Book of Hint

God
is well spoken of by
God

what is evil
what is good
what is

you are
what you are doing

my children are walking
but I
do not imitate
anyone

please send
no help

you know that
God
loves to
stop
by

The Book of J

Jesus Christ
called
to remind you that
you already know all this

Jesus Christ
secretly slipped in among you
long ago

Jesus Christ
a servant
eating with you
at your love feasts
twice dead
flesh
mixed with fear
even the clothes stained

The Book of Relation

your
name will be
water
as clear as
God
flowing
down the middle of the
street

use
these words
for
a lamp
and
look

you are
written

I am
the one who
leaves

Acknowledgments

Thanks to the editors who first published these poems, often in earlier forms, in the following venues:

Amethyst Review: "The Book of Baa," "The Book of Haze," "The Book of What," "The Book of Sin," and "The Book of Lips"

Anomoly Literary Journal: "The Book of Human" and "The Book of This Season"

The Canopy Review: "The Book of Ash" and "The Book of Ear"

The Chaotic Review: "The Book of Numb"

Cobalt: "The Book of Moot"

The Cresset: "The Book of No"

december: "The Book of Help" and "The Book of Relation"

Eunoia Review: "The Book of Evil," "The Book of O," "The Book of Ma," "The Book of Norms," and "The Book of Pain"

Five:2:One: "The Book of On," "The Book of Thirst," "The Book of Seconds," "The Book of Were," and "The Book of Torn Fish"

Gingko Tree Review: "The Book of J"

Heron Tree: "The Book of Ice"

Ink & Letters: "The Book of Us" and "The Book of Cons"

The Nice Cage: "The Book of Peers"

The Other Journal: "The Book of Fists"

Ovenbird Poetry: "The Book of Am"

petrichor: "The Book of Mist" and "The Book of Denial"

Pretty Owl Poetry: "The Book of Coils" and "The Book of Disease"

Psaltery & Lyre: "The Book of Sex," "The Book of Mean," and "The Book of Jam"

Rock & Sling: "The Book of L"

Ryga: "The Book of Class," "The Book of Eke," "The Book of Shoe," "The Book of E," and "The Book of So"

San Diego Reader: "The Book of Calm" and "The Book of Hint"

TAB: A Journal of Poetry & Poetics: "The Book of Genes"

UnLost Journal: "The Book of Icons"

Quail Bell Magazine: "The Book of Dues," "The Book of Thru," "The Book of Hag," "The Book of Same," and "The Book of Respite"

Queen Mob's Tea House: "The Book of Verbs," "The Song of Sons," "The Book of Is," and "The Book of Laminate"

The Windhover: "The Book of Endings"

Thanks also to Tania Runyan for reprinting "The Book of Class" in *How to Write a Form Poem* (T.S. Poetry Press, 2021).

And thanks to Fox Henry Frazier for publishing a small selection of these poems as a chapbook, *A Door with a Voice* (Agape Editions, 2016).

Special Thanks

Thanks to Tom Allbaugh, Diane Glancy, and Christine Kern for surprising me with their laughter and helping me find my direction with their feedback and affirmation in the early days of this project.

Thanks to all of the writers who have written with me, given me feedback, or enthusiastically cheered me on during the making of this book. I'm so fortunate that there are more of you alongside me than I could possibly name on this page, but thanks especially to Emily Capettini, Nicelle Davis, Jen Grace Stewart, Sally Rosen Kindred, Devon Miller-Duggan, Kimbol Soques, Sarah Ann Winn, Tania Runyan, Ki Russell, Elizabeth Dark, Kelly Foster Lundquist, Breeann Kyte Kirby, Robbie Maakestad, Margarita Pintado, Luci Shaw, Eleanor Wilner, my Glen Workshop friends, and all of my Vees.

Thanks also to the PLNU students and alumni who have written with me monthly at Writers Gonna Write as I've finished this manuscript, especially Ellen Huang, Lizzy Kim, Micah Rensunberg, Sarah Morse, and Toby Franklin.

Thanks, always, to my professors and mentors who have also become friends and colleagues: with this project, I'm especially grateful to Carol Blessing, Phil Bowles, Kay Harkins, Doug Harrison, Rick Hill, Karl Martin, Bettina Tate Pedersen, and Marthe Reed for their literary, scholarly, and practical influences, as well as for their encouragement and care.

Thanks to Brenda Martin for inviting me to perform in concert with her, for her collaboration in transforming "The Book of Laminate" into song lyrics, for her incredible jazz improvisations to some of these poems, and for her dear friendship.

Thanks to Point Loma Nazarene University and Azusa Pacific University for supporting this book with awards of time and money.

Thanks to Riot in Your Throat, Crab Orchard, Able Muse, and Green Linden for the finalist, semifinalist, quarterfinalist, and honorable mention nods and encouraging comments on earlier versions of this manuscript.

My profound thanks to Fox Henry Frazier for putting her editorial brilliance to work on these poems and for being so enthusiastic about this project over the last several years.

Thanks to my family members and friends—you know who you are—who have serious (and sometimes funny) conversations with me about important things like misinterpretations and misuses of scripture, faith, and poetry. Let's have more.

Thanks to my parents for giving me my own Bible to read at a young age, taking me to church, and spending years of their lives helping with Bible quizzing; to my Uncle Mike for playfully mixing up Bible stories to make me laugh when I was little; to my church best friend from childhood, Jill Jacobs, for over 30 years of friendship; and to all of my siblings, niblings, grandparents, cousins, aunts, uncles, and friends for your love and support.

Thanks to Elliott and Julian for being your wonderful selves and for loving me so well.

And to Jon: Thank you for supporting me in all things, and thank you for loving me at my most heretical, at my most reverent, and at all points in between.

About the Author

Katie Manning is the founding editor-in-chief of *Whale Road Review* and a professor of writing at Point Loma Nazarene University in San Diego. She is the author of *Tasty Other*, which won the 2016 Main Street Rag Poetry Book Award, and her recent chapbooks include *How to Play* (Louisiana Literature Press, 2022) and *28,065 Nights* (River Glass Books, 2020). Her poems have appeared in *American Journal of Nursing*, *The Lascaux Review*, *New Letters*, *Poet Lore*, and *Verse Daily*, and her poem "What to Expect" was featured on the Poetry Unbound podcast from The On Being Project. Find her online at www.katiemanningpoet.com.

AGAPE
EDITIONS

Agape Editions is a literary micropress created in southern California, now located in upstate New York. We publish visionary literature.

Our name comes from the ancient Greek ἀγάπη (agápē), describing the joyous love that exists universally without seeking or expecting anything in return. Agape can be described as the bond between humans & the Numinous, but we believe it exists everywhere—manifested through the kindness of strangers, felt alone under a sky filled with aurora, made real through a moment of ecstatic meditation or deep connection with another.

A moment of Agape is a moment in which you feel yourself fully—in the broader context of the universe at large.

Agape is about finding the strength & courage to remain open-hearted, in a world that doesn't always encourage or reward an open heart. Our notions of the sacred & the Numinous span wide swaths of experience—private epiphanies; shared ecstasies; moments of intimacy; sublime revelation; cultural identity; spiritual traditions as conduit for survival. The psychic, the occult, the supernatural. The divinity of the natural world. Wild love. Fascinating scientific discovery. Mind-blowing technological advancement. Fernweh. The thrill of exploration. Sacred feminine rage.

We are profoundly uninterested in attempting to dictate the parameters of spiritual experience. We want to feel through you & your writing what's holy to you & why.

Imagine: awakening, breathless, in the thick of night. You've been dreaming of William Blake's Tyger-burning-bright & all its terrifying beauty. & now, from somewhere in the surrounding darkness, you can hear its quiet breathing.

Welcome to Agape Editions.

CPSIA information can be obtained
at www.ICGtesting.com
Printed in the USA
JSHW041509190323
39030JS00009B/19

9 781736 465516